LOVE INTERRUPTED
A Seeker's Discovery of the Afterlife

MICHELE MATTO, M. DIV., M.A.L.A.

Balboa Press books may be ordered through booksellers or by contacting:

Balboa Press
A Division of Hay House
1663 Liberty Drive
Bloomington, IN 47403
www.balboapress.com
1 (877) 407-4847

Names of Mediums in this book have been fictionalized except where individuals gave express permission for their real names to be used.

Unless noted otherwise, all Scripture quotations are taken from the King James Version.

ISBN: 978-1-9822-3139-2 (sc)
ISBN: 978-1-9822-3138-5 (e)

Library of Congress Control Number: 2019909886

Print information available on the last page.

Balboa Press rev. date: 07/24/2019

BALBOA
PRESS
A DIVISION OF HAY HOUSE

Soul mates ultimately are those relationships that assist each individual in his or her spiritual development and the inevitable attainment of wholeness at the level of the soul.

—Kevin J. Todeschi
Edgar Cayce on Soul Mates

Contents

Introduction

I have wanted to write something along the lines of what I jokingly call *Understanding the Afterlife for Dummies* ever since this subject finally started coming together for me. Not because I believe we are dummies—though that would have been a catchy title for this—but because I think there are many people who, like me, have wanted to understand the afterdeath experience and have asked a lot of questions, but they have never received satisfactory explanations from the sources we respected and sought out for answers.

It's not that we don't realize the fact that death is part of life and that we are headed in that direction from birth. But there is a huge difference between the passing of an elderly person, who has lived a full life and worn out the physical body, and when someone unexpectedly or suddenly passes, when a healthy young child dies, or when someone commits suicide. These are the perplexing circumstances that leave many of us asking, "What just happened here, and where are they now? Are they okay? Can someone explain what their new reality is?"

There have been occasional films, such as *Ghost*, that try to portray the afterlife as it is. But often in film and television, the stereotypes of the medium—the person who connects us with our loved ones who have crossed over—are not realistic. The typical portrayals are, at least from my journey and seeking, way off. In my experience with more than fifteen mediums, there have been no Whoopi Goldberg characters (Oda Mae Brown). The mediums I have encountered have looked and acted normal (not gypsy, not flaky, not con artists) and have dressed like the rest of us. They have spoken with an understandable vocabulary and everyday conversation, and they have had (or used to have) "real" jobs: an electrical engineer whose day job is installing landing systems at major US airports, a flight attendant, a former Roman Catholic nun, a holistic nurse, a maintenance man at my summer cottage community, a chef, a court reporter, and a former EMT. It has been surprising and refreshing to discover that mediums are woven into the fabric of society just like the rest of us.

In short, over the past two years, I have learned so much through this journey (which I never learned in seminary) that it has evolved my entire spirituality, expanded my understanding of why we are here, clarified my beliefs about reincarnation, and ultimately provided me with what I call a "grown-up cosmology." When I speak about cosmology, I am referring to time, space, frequency, and vibration—where heaven is and so forth.

It is my hope that what follows here, in words and photos, can help you find your way through the maze that we call the afterlife, and it can do so in a way that finally makes some sense and helps to bring you more clarity. It's not a subject that any of us on this side will ever really understand. But it is possible to be less confused and more at peace with not only where our loved ones are but where we are headed as well.

Along the journey, there will be many seeming contradictions: for one, that which is beyond logic and analysis is nonetheless quite intelligently designed and teaches us much about quantum physics, frequency, and vibration. It also seems contradictory that a realm in which there is no longer time and space is, nevertheless, the place from which we came to earth and the place to which we will return. And finally, eternity is a very long time. Instead of being confused, I now find it all to be quite fascinating, even without having all of the answers!

So here I share my journey with one particular individual—my soul mate—whose transition to the other side I have followed for the past two years. It is she, in fact, who urged me—through four different mediums in four different states—to write down the ways in which my journey of discovery about the afterlife have impacted not only me but also our friends, neighbors, and others along the way.

I will not be using the term "soul mate" as many people in our culture think of it today: as being the other half of you with whom you ride off into the sunset, happily ever after. I use the term in the way Edgar Cayce and other spiritual writers have used it historically, to mean the person in whose presence, and in relationship with whom, each person is somehow propelled toward their own deeper spiritual growth toward wholeness.

"Through an ongoing process of relationships, experiences, and various lifetimes, the soul finds itself involved in a curriculum of personal growth and development," writes Kevin J. Todeschi (*Edgar Cayce on Soul Mates: Unlocking the Dynamics of Soul Attraction*, ARE Press, 1999, xix). It is not a relationship defined or limited by gender or race, or one that fits any of the many boxes into which society wants to place us. This relationship, for both Jenny and me, has been exactly the kind of curriculum of personal growth and development that is more easily seen and understood to be such in her afterlife than was obvious during our physical lives.

CHAPTER 1
Wow! Who Are You?

"If you ever make us wait like this again, you'll find we've left when you get here!"

Little did I realize on that ordinary Sunday, as I arrived late to the administrative board meeting for the twelve-step church I'd created, that I was being addressed by my soul mate, a brilliant high school math teacher, four years my junior, who would forever change my earthly life, my spirituality, and my understanding of why we're here.

I should have been embarrassed and defensive—even angry—since I was late because a parishioner had stopped me to ask for financials, but instead I found my reaction to be fascination with her direct and honest expression of feelings. *Wow! Who are you?* Over the next several years, I would find out.

I don't even remember where that day fits into the chronology of the twenty-four years we would eventually have together. I know that Jennifer Young was referred to my church by the assistant superintendent of the central Ohio school district where she had taught math and computer programming for twenty years. Arnie, Jenny's good friend, as well as the assistant superintendent, had come to our church to visit and stayed. He later suggested to Jenny that she, too, would appreciate the kind of Jungian teachings I brought to adult education each week following worship. Jenny had been raised Roman Catholic and sometimes attended Mass, but mainly she was a so-called fallen-away Catholic.

Even though ours was a small United Methodist ministry of seventy-five to one hundred people, which had space in an existing Methodist church, I somehow really hadn't noticed Jenny. This initially was an experimental outreach, and people came and went; many were professionals who, even if they stayed, weren't always there. We had school psychologists, teachers, former ministers, a psychiatrist, and several health care professionals. Later, when telling our story, I would begin, "In 1993, when I met Jenny ..." and she would correct me with her inimitable math teacher need for correct facts and detail: "I was here in 1991," she'd say with a little snark added for emphasis.

I do recall that, in March 1993, I still did not know her well because my father died March 9, and I was surprised and touched that she attended his weekday afternoon funeral on the far east side of Columbus, Ohio, a thirty-minute drive from our church. He was in the early stage of Alzheimer's and had wandered off from his home in the snow. The helicopters and search-and-rescue dogs found him in a snow bank two days later, not far from his home.

Jenny had taken a leave of absence from teaching math at her district's high school in order to finish her dissertation on leadership and public policy at Ohio State University, and we finally got acquainted when she asked to interview me for a section on "The Spiritual Life of the Leader." The ministry I had created as a special appointment by Bishop Edsel Ammons of the West Ohio Conference was a rather innovative approach to helping adult children of alcoholics (ACOAs) and other codependents to find spirituality in the church. That was, in fact, our fledgling ministry's logo: "Finding Spirituality in Religion."

The idea for this twelve-step approach to religion came together for me near the end of seminary in 1987. I began to realize that the language of that program, the language of Carl Jung and Thomas Merton about the false self versus the true self, and the theology we had been learning, intersected in one authentic spirituality, with or without a particular label.

I had chosen a path in seminary focusing on prayer, spiritual formation, and spiritual direction, all of which fell under the Master of Arts in Liturgical Arts (MALA) degree. I went to Bishop Ammons near the time of my graduation to present my thoughts about all of this and to ask him to consider a specialized ministry for those who were disaffected from the church because of their earlier backgrounds.

Crucial to what I had discovered to be the authentic life of prayer was the discovery of the place where both Eastern and Western thought meet: in the simple acceptance of what is, without judgment. In twelve-step terminology, this would be the fourth step, taking a fearless inventory of ourselves—that is, looking at whatever you find without judgment, much like searching for a can of peas on the grocery store shelf, neither fearful nor overly impressed with what you find: it's just peas on the shelf. This is the underpinning of the ministry idea I presented to the bishop and how I tried to live my own life as well. Now, Jenny wanted to understand more about it all and how it came together in this particular ministry.

Jenny and I met a few times for breakfast at Bob Evans and began sharing our respective ACOA and twelve-step backgrounds and experiences. She brought me a thin hardcover book to our first breakfast, and I remember immediately feeling like a person, not just a minister, as I flipped through it. I don't even recall the title now, though I can still see its light-green cover with a fern on the front in my mind's eye. Clearly, by her selection, she already had a pretty good read on who I was.

When, through our conversations, I began to discern who Jenny Young was as a person, I told her, "I don't think I want to be a subject for your dissertation. I'd rather just be your friend." For one thing, I had discovered that we shared a similar ethic, which is difficult to find in friends. My ethics professor in seminary had pulled me aside one day after class and suggested I could "loosen up" my ethic a bit. Here at Bob Evans was a kindred spirit. I dropped out of the interviews, and we switched gears to develop a friendship instead.

I soon discovered that Jenny's penchant for detail had her somewhat stuck in the writing of her dissertation—too many trees to see the forest, so to speak. And because her PhD advisors in this area of education she had created for herself encouraged collaboration as important to the process, I offered to help her get unstuck. As many of our friends would remark at her Celebration of Life service in April 2017, this was one of many areas in which we "filled each other's holes" as several people wrote on sympathy cards at that time.

Jenny invited me to help her enter data on her little 1993 Apple home computer with a nine-inch screen; she even had to teach me how to use a computer. At the time, I was still writing my sermons longhand on yellow legal paper.

So together we began to wade through the "ditra," as she called it, and she began to get going on the writing. The first time we got together to work, the brown wooden paneling on her family room walls was plastered with fifty three-by-five index cards and Post-it notes with bits of information she'd gathered but hadn't found places yet in the larger scheme.

I had learned, during our breakfasts, where this dissertation was generally headed and what the point was, but as I looked around the family room and read all the cards, I couldn't find any sign of that. I finally blurted out in my inimitable, bull-in-a-china-shop style, "Well, first of all, nobody gives a flying flip about eighty percent of this minute detail. I understand it's supportive and reflects your research, but don't let it pull you off to the side from where you're going with it all."

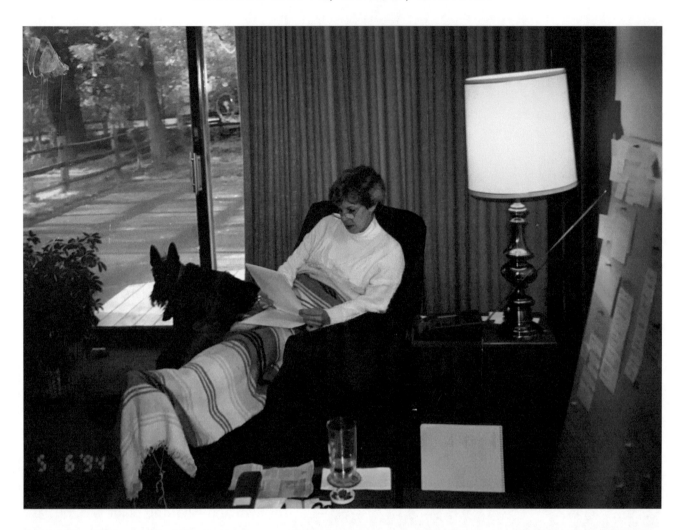

Jenny was probably as shocked by my directness as I had been with hers that Sunday at the church, but you would never know it by looking at her. She was so low key and nonreactive. Yet, through all the years of our long friendship, directness was a common and ongoing thread we both needed from and appreciated in each other. Say what you mean, and mean what you say. Otherwise, relationships are entirely too complicated.

We respected and appreciated each other's journeys and spirituality—whatever those had been and wherever they seemed to be evolving—and we began to tiptoe into sharing those depths with each other as we worked, entering data and moving me into the computer age.

By this time, the congregation was discovering and appreciating Jenny's administrative and communication skills as we began the process of moving from our identity as an experimental outreach to becoming a church, with all that entails. The parishioners were ready to stop being someone's "mission" and to start taking responsibility for our share of conference apportionments and creating our own mission and direction.

The people elected Jenny to the Pastor-Parish Relations Committee (PPR), which is Methodism's way of helping parishioners to understand where the pastor is coming from, and vice versa. Jenny's position on this committee turned out to be the basis for us to develop a deeper friendship because, in that capacity, it was her role to help me sort through some difficult external church staff dynamics that were, administratively and personally, way over my head. So just as the dissertation work had helped me get to see and know the real Jenny and her vulnerabilities, sorting out these issues helped her to see and know the real me and my vulnerabilities.

This specialized ministry placed a high value on having its pastor walk the talk. Therefore, it sent me, along with Jenny as chair of PPR, to continuing education events so we could bring back and teach what we learned and share it with everyone in adult education following worship.

In those days, the teachings that dovetailed with what I had learned in seminary and what Jenny wanted to learn to apply to school systems, centered around how our stress levels and unresolved family-of-origin issues create illness and get in our way, overburdening and breaking down the immune system. Today, this is called behavioral medicine and psychoneuroimmunology. Psychoneuroimmunology, according to Wikipedia, is the "study of the interaction between psychological processes and the nervous and immune systems of the human body." Behavioral medicine takes these understandings about health and illness and applies them to prevention and diagnosis. That's really the long and the short of it.

During these continuing education events we attended, Jenny and I learned that we made great traveling companions and could be quite comfortable sitting together for hours in silence. The summer offerings at the Cape Cod Institute (founded in 1980 by Gilbert Levin, PhD, while a professor at the Albert Einstein College of Medicine), for example, were held at Nauset High School from 9:00 a.m. until noon, with the rest of the day free, but the content was mind-boggling and complex. At that time, Mona Lisa Schulz, a neuropsychiatrist and medical intuitive, was a faculty member who explained to us that researchers had now mapped specifically which spinal nerves were affected by which unresolved emotions. So, anger would land here in the body, regret would be found here, resentment would go there, and so on. Today this is all old news, but at the time, it was a lot to take in. You can find Schulz's writings today on Amazon; she has collaborated with Louise Hay on several books available there.

After the sessions, Jenny and I would get simple peanut butter sandwiches from the Box Lunch, a place in nearby Eastham that prepared food and packaged it to take to the beach. We would drive back past the high school, out to the Nauset seashore, and sit quietly for the rest of the afternoon, thinking about what we had learned in the morning meant for families, for schools, for churches and congregations, and for hospitals. We couldn't have asked for a more beautiful setting to ponder such weighty subjects, and we generally sat there the entire afternoon until dinnertime without saying five words to each other.

CHAPTER 2

Meanwhile, Back at the Ranch ...

Meanwhile, during these years, I was married and raising four kids, mostly teenagers or young adults by this time. The twins were finishing college and then heading to graduate school as the younger two finished high school.

Jenny and my youngest son, Aaron, struck up a particularly close relationship that flourished for as long as Jenny's and mine did. He called as I was writing this, on what would have been her seventieth birthday, to reminisce about some trips we took to her home state of Wisconsin. There they had swung out over Waterville Lake near Oconomowoc on giant rope swings and gone tubing behind Jenny's family's motorboat.

Aaron was eleven when Jenny came into our family. He would call her for company when my husband, Ed, and I went out to dinner, and she would help him with his homework, especially his math. She would tell the story of how they might be on the phone for two hours, but as soon as he heard our car in the driveway, Aaron would say, "Okay, they're home. Bye!"

That cracked up all of us.

Jenny came down to our house and often helped Aaron with his school projects; I teared up sometimes watching the two of them together. For someone who had never had children of her own, Jenny had such a way with them—even teenagers—and infinite patience. She helped us all understand each other.

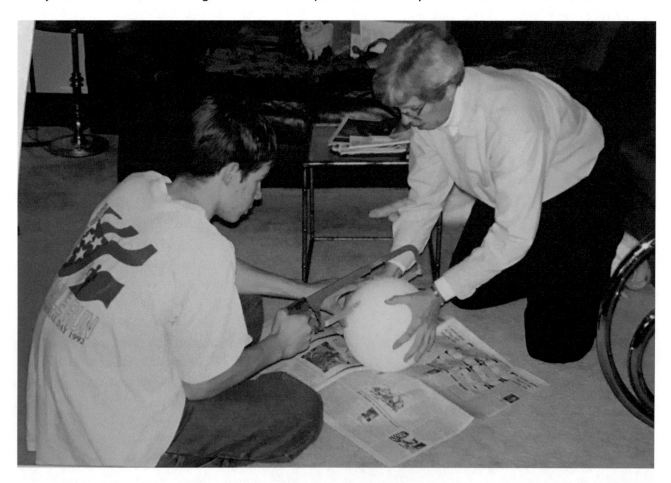

I felt a strong soul connection to Jenny and, living up in my head as I so often had in my lifetime, I tried hard to figure it out. It was many faceted. She was bright and funny, articulate, honest, clear, and direct, but still tactful, gracious, kind, and humble—the most Christ-like person I have probably ever known. And always, on PPR, Jenny encouraged me to be in touch with and express my feelings and be true to myself.

We were both workaholics. They say that when you grow up in an alcoholic family, you'll develop some addiction, and if the addiction isn't to drugs or alcohol, it will likely be to a food or a process, such as working or spending/shopping. My congregation was composed primarily of adults who identified with one or another of these process addictions.

We all knew we needed to learn how to play, and Jenny and I made a commitment to go to a Friday afternoon movie at three o'clock once or twice a month so I could still be home when Aaron arrived from school.

The first time we tried to carve out an afternoon to do that, we were to meet at the local theater at three thirty for the new Nick Nolte film, *The Prince of Tides*. Our treasurer stopped by just as I was heading out the door and needed to ask a couple of quick questions, so I was late and got there about three forty. Expecting to be met by frustration and a reprimand from someone who placed a high priority on punctuality, instead, as I pulled up, there was Jenny with our tickets in hand, waiting for me graciously—no lecture, no reprimand. She had trusted that I would show up and had done what she needed to so we could have our afternoon off—not that *The Prince of Tides* was the most relaxing movie I'd ever seen. But I was so touched by simply being understood and not having to explain.

On other Fridays, we took our three Samoyeds—I had Bear and Kodi, and Jenny had Casey—to Old Man's Cave in the Hocking Hills of southern Ohio and hiked or talked. One Good Friday I took her through Sugar Grove, Ohio, to show her my church camp—Camp Akita, meaning "the searcher"—that had been so meaningful and influential in my childhood.

I was stressed in those days, trying to make the church and family at home fit into the twenty-four hours we are given. Jenny was always asking, "What do *you* want?" To this day, remembering that brings tears to my eyes. She was so kind, gracious, and funny, and she never said a bad word about anyone. I used to joke that Jenny could call you a horse's ass, and you would walk away smiling.

On our way to meetings, I often relayed to her what I wanted to say, and she would translate it into language that could better be heard. If I really felt like saying, "We need to get off the dime here and just do something," Jenny would translate that, after first patiently waiting for the right time in the meeting, to say, "Time is of the essence now, and we need to move forward with what we've said we want." Sometimes I could hardly recognize the gracious ideas that my original thoughts had become!

Jenny arranged, with her other assistant superintendent, for me to sit in on the district's offering to its staff of Steven Covey's *The Seven Habits of Highly Effective People*. She taught me some neurolinguistic programming, which was the major content of her dissertation, and explained outcome specification, where you begin with what you hope to accomplish in the end and then work backward on how to get there. She also taught me the finer points of clarifying objectives.

I helped her finish typing and entering data for her dissertation, and Dr. Jennifer Ann Young received her PhD in December 1994 from The Ohio State University. We took a short, free cruise to the Bahamas, which I had won at the local jazz and rib festival. It had been the carrot on a stick when she felt bogged down along the way. I had put a picture of the tropics on her computer screen and left it there for months as an incentive to get 'er done.

Over the next few years, spiritual direction urged me to get out of my head more and follow my heart. When my director, by this time a Jungian analyst who had left the priesthood and faculty of a Catholic seminary and gone to Zurich to study Jung, first told me to follow my heart, I had no idea what he meant. Honestly. I was so focused on the intellect, and intellect also had drawn me to my husband back when I was seventeen.

Somewhere along the way—it took me about eight years to even begin to figure out what kind of relationship Jenny and I had— I remember asking Dick, the Jungian analyst, about the connection I felt toward Jenny. "What is this?" I said as I described the ways I was growing toward all that she represented and who she was.

After listening, Dick finally said, "I don't know what it is either, but what I do know is that you will tear the fabric of your soul if you do not let it just evolve and see for yourself what it is to be."

Ironically, in one of my one-on-one sessions with the therapist Ed and I had been seeing for counseling at the time, I asked her the same question. Her response was almost identical to Dick's: "You will do violence to your soul if you extinguish it out of fear."

Jenny and I felt and believed that the spiritual connection we had transcended sexuality, and we were not going to allow whatever we had to be trivialized by placing it into the convenient box society would like to choose for us. Back in seminary, we had learned that sexuality is on a continuum and much more fluid than most people realize or want to admit. So, I had already, at that time, moved away from believing that any of us really fit into one box or another. I was fine with whatever my own truth was going to be, but it had to be my truth, not anyone else's, and certainly not one that simply made it convenient for outsiders to not have to think very deeply.

In retrospect, I *was* definitely feeling a strong soul connection to Jenny, but my spiritual beliefs had not yet caught up with my reality. It felt sacred is all I could grasp, and that had to be enough. I was fortunate to have had excellent spiritual direction and Jungian analysis throughout those eight years or so.

By 1999 my mother had died, and I took a leave of absence to execute her estate and clear my head. Ed and I began to separate, divorcing in 2001. Our counseling had begun before I graduated from seminary. We were growing in different directions and had major differences about how to spend our discretionary time and vacations and about parenting our four kids. Seminary, as well as all these continuing education learnings, had definitely changed me; I'll agree with that. It was almost as if the more we actually heard each other in counseling, the more the handwriting was on the wall that we were no longer in alignment.

The leave of absence gave me the space to clarify my values and thinking. I established a private practice in Spiritual Direction (the name given to the practice of simply sitting with people and listening as they focus intentionally on their spiritual growth) for a couple of years and led some weekend retreats at my childhood church camp, Akita, while I thought about what I wanted now for me.

My grandparents had lived on the east coast of Florida when I was growing up, and we went down most every winter. Now, decades later, I came in from shoveling a heavy, wet April snow one day and opened up the computer to find an AOL questionnaire on "Best Places to Retire." Aaron was now in college in Indiana, and when he did come home, he spent most of his time up at Ohio State seeing old friends. I asked myself, *Why am I here shoveling snow and schlepping mulch when nobody's home?* So, I sat down and answered the retirement questions. Four places emerged from my responses, three of which were within two hours of each other on the west coast of Florida: Bradenton, Port Charlotte, and Punta Gorda.

In 2002, I called and asked Jenny if she wanted to go with me on Memorial Day weekend to check out these places. If we combined our households—sharing my house in Florida in the winters and hers in Ohio in the summers—we could have the best of both worlds with no real sacrifice financially. We each had our own house anyway. By now Jenny was a year from retirement as an assistant principal at a large and progressive new suburban high school in her district, for which she had done the site study for its building. She said, "I can't go to Florida over Memorial Day weekend! We have high school graduation, and I have teacher

evaluations to finish. The only way I can go is if you're willing to fly."

So, I did. We fell in love with Port Charlotte, I put 10 percent down on a house to build in a gated community called Riverwood, and we never looked back. Until the day Jenny died, every time we drove into Riverwood, she exclaimed what a beautiful environment we had created for our retirement years. It was a golf course community, and she usually had won a prize for the longest drive during the high school staff golf outings, but by now we weren't playing. Jenny loved all the space a golf course creates around a housing development. And space we had! As we drove up a small hill and over the rise, looking out over the clubhouse and fairways, we looked at each other and exclaimed, "I could do this!"

In 2003, the house was finished, Jenny had retired, and we moved on January 25. It was everything we loved: simple and small enough to be cost efficient but large enough to not be claustrophobic. It looked out over our pool and a small lake beyond. This was our retreat house. The west coast of Florida— the quiet coast—is the last bastion of fishing and relatively low traffic and density. I still live there, exactly where Walt Disney had been planned to go in, back in the 1950s; however, the airport was not sufficient, so Disney World went instead to Orlando. The roads around Riverwood, where I now live, are all paved and named, but nobody's home!

By 2005 we downsized from Jenny's large house in Ohio to a smaller condo, and eventually a few years later, we sold that to build a summerhouse on Lake Gaston on the North Carolina/Virginia border. A friend of hers from their thirty years of teaching together had moved there with her husband. We lived there five summers, learning how to play—taking cruises to Alaska, where we went on a dog sled excursion; to Mexico, where we trained dolphins; and later to Italy, where we took a fresh look at her original Catholic church. But mostly, we went jet-skiing around Lake Gaston, lunched with her teacher friends, and enjoyed my new grandkids, who all came along in those years.

As we got older, the Jet Skis and pontoon boat were too much for us to schlep on and off the trailers, and even though this was Jenny's favorite house, we knew it was time to let it go before we were not able to maintain it properly. It was in a heavily wooded area, and we had chainsawed the trees and pruned the vines to create a nice tick-free clearing, but this was an hour from the nearest good hospital, and we were getting older.

We built an eight-hundred-square-foot condo cottage in southern coastal Maine, where we spent what would turn out to be the last two summers of Jenny's life. The cottage was a smaller version of our Florida house, a mile and a half from the ocean, and it was quiet once we got off Route 1. In the summers, we loved our little creation, even though it was somewhat crowded with our four dogs—now our Samoyeds, Trek, Muf'n, and Canai, and our golden retriever, Chance. But home was always Riverwood in Florida, where we lived until March 3, 2017, when our lives together were rudely interrupted.

CHAPTER 3
Love Interrupted

On March 1, 2017, it was a beautiful, warm, sunny Florida morning, like most every day at that time of year—certainly why we moved there. Jenny always took the dogs out, one by one, while I started their breakfasts. But on this morning, I was taking our new show puppy, TJ, outside too, so we were out there together along the side of the house.

Jenny said to me, "I think it's chilly today. Are you cold?"

"No, I'm not," I replied.

And this was the beginning of the end. Love interrupted, rudely interrupted.

We had had almost perfect health for decades. Jenny had smoked for twenty-five years before I met her, and I had to be careful with my own lungs, so when we combined our households, I said, "I can't live with a smoker. I inhaled enough secondary smoke from my dad for a lifetime, growing up. Do you think you can stop for our health?" And she did. She had a couple of initial relapses, but she was committed to stopping, and she did.

Nevertheless, that was the "other shoe" I was waiting to drop during all our years together because there was no shortage of information about how smoking causes long-term effects that can show up years later. But we were not prepared for what this was going to be.

Jenny continued to feel cold, and by 8:00 a.m. I was driving her to the hospital. On the way I remember asking, "Do you want me to go to (a larger city's) hospital?" But that was out of network for her retirement insurance plan. I had taken her there for a sliced finger once when we were woodcarving, and it became the $1,000 sliced finger.

So, she said, "No, just go to our hospital." And in the end, I suppose it wouldn't have made a difference.

All of the tests she had that fateful morning came out okay. An intake ER nurse did call a "sepsis alert," but she told me that she didn't want me to worry; she just did that to get people moving quickly on whatever this was. The strep test, flu test, all the usual things came back negative, and she was discharged about 12:30 p.m. with a diagnosis of virus—"Go home and take Tylenol." The nurse gave me a sheet with five conditions; if any returned, she was to come back.

Jenny walked into the pharmacy with me to get the Tylenol, which we don't even keep in the house, and spent the afternoon visiting with friends from our Virginia neighborhood, who had just arrived at lunchtime. We went to the Riverwood Grill where Jenny had her usual club sandwich, and it would be her last meal.

By 5:00 p.m., Jenny was on the couch watching our recording of the new *Dancing with the Stars* cast, announced that day on *Good Morning America*. I recall our puppy, TJ, jumping up on her and landing on her chest, and she didn't even complain or yell at him.

We decided to go to bed early, and by nine o'clock, we each took two Advil PMs and settled down for a good night's sleep. But around four in the morning she was up and sick, and by eight, when I heard anything, she was clearly having two of the symptoms on the list they had handed me. She was getting weak and hadn't been able to keep down the Gatorade I'd picked up at the gas station before bed, so I figured she had to be getting dehydrated.

I said, "You need to get back to the hospital." She did not want me to call the squad, but she seemed to be getting so weak that I wasn't sure I could manage if I had to lift her. We were about fifteen pounds different in weight. She insisted I just drive her there.

By the time we arrived at the emergency room on March 2, she looked very sick. As I look back, knowing what I now know, this was septic shock, and everything was going to hell. When we arrived, her blood pressure was 50/39. The staff started fluids and brought up her blood pressure. Still, she had no other symptoms they could pinpoint, and it was after noon when an abdominal ultrasound showed a gall bladder infection, so it needed to come out. She was in no shape to undergo surgery, and her platelets were low, but I think we all knew there was no other course of action. So we agreed, and they took her in by 2:00 p.m.

Jenny was in there for six hours. Our friends who had arrived the day before came to the hospital and brought me some dinner. Finally, the critical care specialist, who happened to also be my pulmonologist when I'd needed a C-PAP the year before, came to ask my permission to insert an access line into her carotid artery. He did not mince words: "There isn't time to explain it all; I need to do this." He's an excellent doctor, and I trusted his judgment.

After Jenny was moved from recovery to the ICU upstairs, I was allowed to go up. It was almost 8:00 p.m., and she looked puffy and not like Jenny at all. I sat with her, not knowing if she was able to hear me or take in anything.

At this time, I had no personal experience with death and dying. My mom had had a stroke during the night and was gone when we found her the next morning. My dad had been found two days later after he'd walked off from his house. Jenny's parents had died before we met. My congregation had two people hospitalized in ten years and no deaths.

My middle son, Kevin, who lived in Connecticut, texted me while I was in the surgical waiting room and asked if he could come down. I couldn't even think straight. Make reservations for a plane flight and what? When would that be? And take off work? I don't think I even gave him an answer. He flew down on NetJets and arrived around 9:00 p.m. He stayed with Jenny while I went home and put the four dogs to bed, turned out the lights, and covered their beds as usual, pretending to them that everything was normal.

The ICU nurse called and asked if I wanted to get back there because Jenny was losing heart rate, blood pressure, everything. I said yes, but I don't remember what happened next. I think I went back at 9:30 or 10:00… but came home to sleep at eleven. I just remember Kevin coming into my room at about 5:00 a.m., waking me, and saying, "We need to go back to the hospital. Do you want to go together?" I was in a sleepy haze, and he was impatient with that and said, "Just meet me there."

Driving over, I received a voice mail from the nurse with her direct callback number, so I hit "call back," and she answered. She asked if I had talked to my son. I told her he came into my room and said we had to go back to the hospital. "I'm on my way now," I said. She asked, "But did you talk to him?" I guessed I hadn't really. I know I was in shock about how fast this had all proceeded since being on the beach just the day before. She explained that Jenny had coded, and they tried twice to revive her, but she died at—what? Like 5:30 a.m. Gone. Love interrupted, rudely Interrupted. We weren't ready. And neither of us had been there with her.

We were just saying on the way to the pharmacy how we'd had many years of good health, and we hadn't been sitting around searching online for all the illnesses we could get as we neared our seventies. When the nurse had told me that she had called a "sepsis alert," I thought she'd said "substance alert" since the whole country is overdosing these days. And I had told her, "Well, I can *guarantee* you Jenny is not on crack!" Little did I know. Her gall bladder, when they did get it out, was gangrenous, and she died of septic shock.

I absolutely could not compute all this. Does anyone in America in 2017 get gangrene? Has anyone on this side of *Saving Private Ryan* gotten gangrene? All of our continuing education events on Cape Cod, our seminars with distinguished medical school faculty, and the psychoneuroimmunology conferences at Hilton Head on mind/body/spirit connections … but you can have essentially no symptoms until twenty-four hours before you're dead?

The day before we were standing in the yard with the dogs, we had gone to Englewood Beach for lunch with friends visiting from Maine. They were all walking the beach while I went to fetch the car. That was February 28. And by early morning of March 3 she was gone.

CHAPTER 4
Wait Just a Damn Minute!

During the next couple of weeks, all four of my adult children flew to Florida, juggling child care as needed, and were there for either the celebration of Jenny's life service we created at Riverwood, or the next week when school was out for spring break. While they were there, of course, there was so much to attend to—deciding where to eat meals, exercising the four dogs, making all the arrangements, and so forth – that it was kind of surreal. I obviously knew intellectually that Jenny was gone, but there was no time to process emotions.

I remember coming home one noontime from the funeral home and seeing Kevin and Coleen, Jenny's longtime friend from Wisconsin, walking down the street toward home with all four dogs in tow. They had decided to walk the four fifty-pound Samoyeds together, something Jenny and I never dared to do with all the wildlife, and even just the squirrels, around Riverwood.

The funeral director had given me permission to bring the dogs in early on Saturday morning before a family viewing but said only immediate family could be present. My three sons and I took the dogs in one at a time to let them see and sniff Jenny in the casket so they could try to grasp that she was now different. The little ones, two and three years old, were—like little children—not getting it. But Trek, whom Jenny had always bathed and groomed for his dog shows, was now seven, and he was on hyperalert. He went first to one shoulder and then around to her other shoulder. You could see his little wheels turning in his white furry head: *What's happening here? This is Mommy Jen, but she is really different.*

Jenny was cremated, and Aaron's fiancée had a friend make a wooden box for her ashes so I could have the top carved. One of our woodworking mentors carved on the lid, a picture from a photo at Acadia National Park that we always loved: Jenny leaning against a boulder at Otter Point with Trek. On the sides he carved

two dolphins from our trip to Mexico, with her name and dates of her birth and death. After Ron carved the scenes, I painted them to match the photos. It is still so meaningful. It was everything our life together was: our enjoyment of nature and hiking, our love of the ocean and water, and the kinship we felt with animals, the outdoors, our dogs, and each other—all carved by a friend.

Before I left Florida to go to Maine for the summer, I began traditional grief counseling because I knew what the emotional trajectory was going to be. I even found a twelve-step certified chemical dependency counselor (CCDC), a therapist who was familiar with the kind of work I'd done so I didn't have to start at the beginning with our story. But traditional grief counseling was not going to help me, and I have since learned that it is not helpful for so many people. (See *Love Knows No Death*, by Piero Calvi-Parisetti, MD, chapter 3, "Helpful and Less Helpful Approaches.")

I remember taking to one of our sessions a copy of Jenny's undergraduate thesis for her mathematics degree, "Wave Motion and Acoustical Analysis," which I had found while looking in the den for a photo frame. I had never heard her mention it in all our years together.

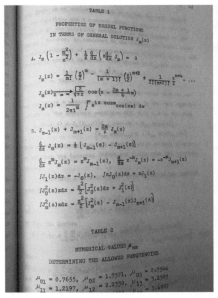

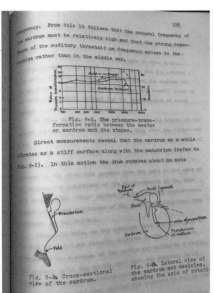

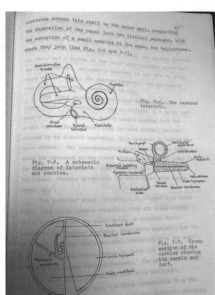

I said to the grief therapist, "What makes me so extraordinarily depressed about Jenny's death is that she was just, all in one person, so brilliant, kind, caring, gracious, and funny but, at the same time, so understated. Neighbors stopped me on my walks with our dogs after reading her obituary to say they'd had no idea that she had a PhD or had accomplished so much. There will just never be another Jenny Young."

The therapist replied, "No, there won't."

I can think of at least three responses that would have been really helpful had I been on the ministerial end of this kind of conversation in my own office, but this reply was none of those.

I probably got more benefit from going back to the hospital in April to discuss why they didn't start her on antibiotics the first day and figure out later if she needed them. Since the intake ER nurse had called a "sepsis alert," someone must have thought that was a possibility. Why wouldn't you give antibiotics first and decide later if they were needed?

The medical representative had Jenny's entire chart both on the table before him and memorized in his head for our appointment. I wanted medical facts and information, but I was calm and reasoned, not angry. I hoped this representative would have gray hair and a lot of experience, and not be twenty-five years old. I was pleasantly surprised on all fronts. He was at least fifty, he had done his homework, and he was quite convincing.

He said they finally determined after the fact that the bacteria she had was *chryseobacterium indologenes*. No hospital, even a larger city hospital like Tampa General or Sarasota, would have given the antibiotic effective against this strain of bacteria without knowing its specific name on that first day. Even Levaquin, a powerful drug I've taken for "hot tub lung" is not effective against this strain. In addition, the sepsis marker on that first day was not there. I forget the number, but it has to be maybe eight-plus, and her number was only 5.4 or something. It's a blur now, but at the time, our longtime friend Mary, a nurse and former parishioner, was in Florida and went over the medical charts with me to help me understand it all. I left the hospital this time feeling that the staff had done everything they could do.

By May I dropped out of the unhelpful counseling, left our home in Florida, and took the dogs and Jenny's ashes in our RV to our cottage in Maine.

CHAPTER 5
Finding a Connection

Once I was settled in Maine, I knew I had to keep doing my personal work, and I set up appointments first with the wonderful and skilled massage therapist we had up there. I trusted her and figured that like many of these integrative health practitioners, she was probably connected to a community of healers in the area. I told her after all the mind/body/spirit education Jenny and I had done, I still couldn't get my head around how she could have no symptoms that the doctors could use to make an intelligent diagnosis until it was too far down the pike.

I said, "Jenny is the only person who has the answers to the questions I have." I asked if she knew any good mediums who could connect me with those who have crossed over to the other side. I knew there were some but nothing else about the subject. The church has traditionally controlled how we see the afterlife by urging "faith alone," so there was no education along those lines in seminary. When people came into my office for answers to questions like "Do you believe in reincarnation?" I answered honestly, "This life is taking all my energy. I don't have any left over to figure out the last one or the next one." Funny but true, really. So, I was just like every other lay person in my understanding of the afterlife. Yes, we will meet up again some day with our loved ones, but when and where exactly?

The resurrection and the entire Easter event are the linchpin of the Christian faith, and if people can't in some way get their heads around that, they really aren't Christians. So, we all pretty much *do* believe Jesus rose from the dead and that Mary and the women saw him—everything we hear each year at Easter. But the artwork is pretty rudimentary. Do we really think he flew up in the sky? Come on. The church really needs a grown-up cosmology. And I was about to receive just that, but not in the way they taught in catechism.

I told Annie (my massage therapist), "If I'm going to do this, I need to see a good one. I can't afford to be any more confused!"

The world of television mediums and shows about them had not been my world. At this exact time, I was trying to order a book called *Good Grief* that we used to help bereaved people, but on Amazon that book I had given away when I left the ministry was no longer even in print. There was, however, a newer book with that same title by Theresa Caputo, so I ordered it. This was the first I had heard of her or her television show doing exactly this kind of mediumistic work with people.

As in the movie *Ghost*, however, something gets distorted in these television and film productions. I didn't want the Oda Mae Brown effect in my medium. I wanted someone normal. And I wanted Annie to find her for me—preferably in Maine—and sooner rather than later.

Annie gave me several leads, and I went to this bookstore and crystal and metaphysical shop. Jenny had been into this metaphysical stuff back in 1993 when we met, but I was just not there. She used to have a crystal pendant necklace, and I remember jokingly saying to her, "Don't wear that thing around me!" I was suspicious of anyone and anything that purported to manipulate people's energy.

That is why, I think, we agreed to disagree about all that and focused our energies and resources instead on what we could agree on: behavioral medicine and psychoneuroimmunology. Next, we had decided that we needed to learn how to play and lighten up, and we just never got back to the rest of it again.

We did get our aura photographs taken once in 1994 at a psychic fair in Columbus, Ohio, when Kirlian photography was becoming popular.

But generally, I thought that was all pretty "airy-fairy" and needed to stay grounded and solid. Even so, my friends in seminary used to tease me and say I was "so heavenly minded I was no earthly good."

Determined to find an excellent, legitimate medium, but not expecting to find one in Maine, I went online and looked for a famous one at the national level, though hopefully in the eastern half of the country. I had never heard of the Forever Family Foundation, a nonprofit, all-volunteer organization, whose boards are comprised of scientists, researchers, medical doctors, academics, and mediums dedicated to helping people who are dealing with loss and grief come to the understanding that, as they put it, love knows no death.

So, still searching on my own, I watched a YouTube interview in which a medium, whom I'll call Mike, from the Northeast interviewed two newscasters on television, and that was really impressive. You could watch one of them, in real time, go from the beginning of the interview as a skeptic to becoming emotionally charged as Mike laid out the reasons for his friend's recent suicide. This medium, famous or not, was laying out "evidentiary" material (facts and truths that the client will know are actual evidence coming from the loved one in spirit) that even convinced a former skeptic within thirty seconds. Impressive.

I contacted Mike's office and put myself in the queue to have a reading. He was booking about five months out, however, and eventually the date I got was not until November when I would be back home in Florida. Even that only opened up because of a Skype cancellation they'd had a week or two after I left my name. So, I kept looking for something more immediate.

A Jewish musician who was a neighbor in our cottage community stopped me one Saturday on my way to the recycling bin to express his condolences about Jenny's passing. "I want you to know Jenny is here!" he added. "When we drove in the first day this spring, I felt her here and told my wife, 'Jenny's here!'"

I was stunned for several reasons. First, I wasn't expecting to have this conversation with any neighbors, least of all someone from a faith that generally does not include a belief in the afterlife. I was surprised on so many fronts.

He said, "If you ever want to connect with Jenny, I have a guy I went to in Massachusetts, and he's the real deal. If you want to make an appointment, I'll try to find his name again."

He later found the medium's name, and I called and got an appointment for July 24, about six weeks away. Six weeks was better than five months, and he was even a recommendation from someone I knew to be a trustworthy reference.

Still looking, it turned out there was a well-known medium right in my southern coastal area of Maine, and my massage therapist had recommended her, but she was booked out even further than Mike. I did make an appointment with her too, but it wasn't until December 28. So, I kept looking and focused for the time being on paying attention to my body rather than on grief counseling.

CHAPTER 6
Never Say "No, I Don't Think So!" to a Medium!

Because the resurrection is the central element of the Christian faith, it has perplexed me why the church has not done much investigation about the afterlife or supported former members who believe that people who have crossed over are speaking to them, or tried to reconcile the whole subject for us through scripture.

There are billboards all through the Bible Belt (in my own travels, driving from Ohio to Florida on Interstate 75) reminding us of John 3:16: "For God so loved the world, that he gave his only begotten Son, that whosoever believeth in him should not perish, but have everlasting life" (King James Version). I would think that there would be a pretty big teaching emphasis on what that is all about—what it means and how to interpret it.

Instead, exploring the afterlife seems to be taboo, based on old superstitions and historical witch trials—and I'm not even sure what else feeds into the church's position, other than the assumption that maybe we just can't handle the truth. But I'm pretty sure it has to do with controlling what we as parishioners, and even clergy, believe and carry forward with us, rather than the idea that "ye shall know the truth, and the truth shall make you free" (John 8:32 KJV).

I was looking for the answers that only Jenny had to my questions, and I knew there were people who could connect you with those who had crossed over. I just wasn't sure how to go about it or how to know I was seeing a legitimate one. But I knew that people find excellent doctors, lawyers, and roofers by asking their friends or friends of friends. What I didn't know or expect was the extent to which this journey was going to change my present life.

What I learned in the next two years, through my experience with excellent and legitimate mediums providing "evidence" as they call it, not only has totally changed my spirituality, but also has enhanced my understanding of scripture. It has finally provided me the grown-up cosmology I had been searching for since even before seminary. Again, when I speak of cosmology, I am referring to space, time, creation, the laws of physics, and how it all works—where heaven is and so forth.

I met with my first medium in June 2017, on a Saturday morning at nine o'clock. I will call her Judith since this is not intended to be any kind of endorsement of or narrative about local mediums. Her office was in a long, modern office building near McDonald's and the post office in a small Maine town. She was next door to a psychotherapist from whom she rented space. There was no incense burning or any weirdness happening here. She was not strange in any way, not airy-fairy or celestial or wispy. Dressed in a business casual suit, Judith was normal in appearance, and about fifty-five years old, I guessed. I arrived at her office a few minutes early as she was turning on the lights and getting organized. She greeted me with a hug, and said, "Oh my God! You are so sad!" I broke out laughing because I felt that I was in my 9:00 a.m. business persona, so if she thought *this* was sad, she should have seen me back in March and April!

Judith's office was furnished much like a therapist's office: upholstered white sofa, coffee table, and two upholstered chairs facing each other, with soft lighting from lamps on the end tables. I sat at one end of the sofa, and she sat in one of the chairs facing me. As we began, she introduced herself as a "medium, a psychic, and an empath" and tried to explain to me what each of those were.

A medium is able to "read" the energy of people who have crossed over to the other side—what we call dead people, although they are not actually dead but now exist in a changed form of energy. (As Einstein said, "Energy cannot be created or destroyed; it can only be changed from one form to another.")

A psychic "reads" the energy of the "sitter," or client. All mediums are psychic, but not all psychics are mediums. This is important in determining whether you're speaking to a person who is connecting to your loved one or someone who is just reading your energy. If the person can relay information that is evidentiary—evidence only you would know is coming from your loved one—that is mediumistic. If the person is only relaying information he or she is reading off of you, no matter how fascinating or true it is, that is not the loved one speaking to this person; that is *you* "speaking" to him or her.

An empath is someone who can feel your feelings when they are within about three feet of you, even through your coat. I have learned about this as I've gone along and more so in these past several months. But that much got me started on the path to getting answers to my questions about Jenny's death and her present existence.

Judith allowed me to record our session and ask questions. At some points it was almost as if we were having a three-way dialogue between Jenny, Judith, and me. To answer my immediate medical questions, Jenny related that she hadn't thought the initial discomfort she'd been feeling for a few days was any big deal, no more than the lactose intolerance we both experienced, especially rich dairy. I remember asking her on those first couple of days, "Did you take your Lactaid?" But that wouldn't add up to anything like gall bladder infection of the magnitude she had going on.

Additionally, Judith relayed that it was Jenny's nature not to like being the center of attention. Absolutely. She didn't like imposing on people or being made a fuss over, and she knew I would do exactly that, I suppose. The long and the short of it was that she missed the seriousness of this and overestimated her ability to deal with it, despite all our wonderful seminars on mind/body/spirit connections. And by the time she realized she was in trouble, it was way down the pike. Everything Judith communicated to this point was exactly who Jenny was, and this could not be read off of me psychically.

That's the short version. There are a few other nuances: Judith said Jenny had a high pain tolerance as is true of many ACOAs who typically are less in touch with their bodies since they've accommodated to "stuffing" so much from childhood. I used to tease Jenny about running into the cupboards overhead in the RV: "Watch where you're putting your head!"

After about fifteen minutes, when we seemed to have exhausted that topic, Judith said, "But Jenny is saying something else now. She says you are going to be taking another look at ministry and getting into helping others who have experienced grief and lost loved ones—not like a job with hours but you will be doing that."

"No, I don't think so!" I emphatically disagreed. "I'm seventy-two, I'm retired, and I don't need a job."

"Well, I'm just relaying to you what Jenny is saying."

Judith also said that Jenny appreciated the way I rubbed her feet in the hospital when she was so cold and when I went for extra blankets, both of which I did. At one point, she said, "Jenny wants you to pay more attention to what we *have* and never put it in the past as what we *had*. 'I want you to say, "This is what we have, and this is who we are."'

"She says you're having a tough time picking yourself up and moving forward." Judith described our relationship pretty accurately, saying we were like twins in that we finished each other's sentences, and we were comfortable in silence with each other and could sit together quietly for hours. "You two have been in other lives together. You know that, right?"

No, I did not know that. I didn't even know at this time what I really believed about reincarnation, but it would explain a lot of things. And although I couldn't get my head around reincarnation yet, I did have an image one night, while falling off to sleep, of Siamese twins being separated, but not carefully or surgically separated -- they were just being ripped apart.

For the first session I'd ever had with a medium, this was all pretty mind-blowing. First of all, I had never seen a medium aside from Oda Mae Brown in *Ghost*. This was definitely not that. So here was my first real-life medium, and she was not what I had expected. This was the first of many months of "cognitive dissonance" I was about to experience on many different levels.

That first hour went fast, and the next month my nurse friend, Mary, was coming to visit from Columbus, Ohio. She wanted me to make an appointment for her too. I made us back-to-back appointments, and I met Judith for the second time on July 23.

As we drove the thirty minutes up the freeway to Judith's office, I remember that Mary seemed very nervous. I teased her, "What are you uptight about? You afraid she's going to tell you your dad never really loved you?" Mary laughed, and that seemed to have broken the ice. It was all about having no idea what this was going to be like—basically, how weird can it be? I get that!

I parked, introduced Mary to Judith, and then walked over to McDonald's to have breakfast while they met for Mary's hour.

My second session was the game-changer regarding "Are they making this all up, or is this for real?" Judith, part way through my hour, asked, "Do you have a camper? Because Jenny is showing me the wheels of a camper and wants you to check the tires. Something about cracking."

"I have a thirty-two-foot Coachmen Freelander Class C Motor Home. I don't think of it as a camper, but yes, it's what we took the dogs to dog shows in, and we just got this present one in 2015, so it only has twenty-one-thousand miles on it. They're Michelins, so no, I don't think so."

"Well, Jenny is quite insistent about checking the tires," Judith reiterated matter-of-factly. She was clearly accustomed to delivering information people found unbelievable; it was just her job.

"It's up in Saco now getting a new shade for over the sofa. I can have them check the tires before I pick it up."

Seacoast RV called the following day, Monday, and said the shade was installed, and I went to pick up the RV on Tuesday. When I arrived, an employee was sitting on the ground pondering the front left tire. She said the left front tire and the right rear were cracking in the sidewalls. We talked about it awhile, and eventually I wanted to ask someone who really knew tires, *What's the deal here?* I took pictures of the cracks and took the photos up the street to show my Ford dealer.

"Are these cracks important since they're just in the sidewalls?"

"Yes, they are, depending on what you run over and where." His lift was tied up the next week, and I was supposed to take my daughter, her husband, and the grandkids to Acadia on the weekend, so I wanted it checked out at once. He referred me to a commercial tire business in Sanford, closer to our cottage, that specialized in dump trucks and semis, and I drove it over there the next day.

The tire specialist told me not to be surprised if, when they removed the tires, they found cracking on the two inside rear tires as well; that would be likely. I left it there while my friends took me to lunch, and I told the owner to do whatever was necessary. The Ford dealer had seemed to trust this guy.

When we returned after lunch, he said that was exactly what they had found. Four of the six tires were cracking in the sidewalls. It turns out that Michelin tires were known by these tire servicemen to crack in the sidewalls, and since we bought the RV in Florida—and it had been sitting down there for some months between dog shows—that would not be hard to grasp. I would have looked at them in about a year. The RV was five years old, and I would probably have replaced them in six years, regardless of the mileage. What was freaking me out was how could Jenny know any of this? Or how could Judith know any of it?

I was going to struggle for a long time with how people on the other side could see and hear with no eyes and ears. I was at a grief retreat sponsored by the Forever Family Foundation the following January when a respected and certified medium, a former Roman Catholic nun, was doing a reading in our small group breakout session. She was telling one woman, "Your husband says he sees you finally cleaned out the garage!"

Where does this come from? I wondered. I had absolutely no understanding of vibration, and it took me the next two years to even begin to understand how this all worked.

CHAPTER 7
More Craziness, Continued

The next evening, July 24, was the night I'd made the appointment in Massachusetts with Corey, whom my neighbor in Maine had recommended. Mary, my nurse friend, was still visiting, and because it was a ninety-minute drive down there, I said, "I made this appointment before I met Judith; I don't need to see another guy tonight." But Mary insisted, "I'll feed the dogs; you go and see what this one has to say." Mary doesn't believe anything until it's checked out and verified by three witnesses, so she wanted to see if these mediums would say similar things—if they were really speaking with Jenny.

I drove down and met Corey in the same kind of nondescript office building where you might meet with your accountant. He had a large waiting room and a small office with a desk. He sat behind the desk, just as your accountant would, and I sat in front of the desk. Corey was a flight attendant, and once again, I was shocked by how normal and all-American he appeared. He wore a navy-blue hooded sweatshirt, with his airline's logo on the chest, and khaki pants; his haircut was very short, almost a buzz cut. There was nothing airy-fairy here, just a soft-spoken, gentle guy, maybe thirty-five years old.

He worked a little differently from Judith. He requested that I bring a photo of my loved one. So, I brought one of my favorite pictures of Jenny—purposely without the dogs—standing at the base of the waterfall in the town center of Camden, Maine, and he began immediately: "This person did not have to pass. I don't want to say she was misdiagnosed because that's not quite correct. It is that she didn't have any symptoms they could pinpoint until it was too late. But her passing was unnecessary."

I was blown away. I was just figuring that out around this time. His analysis of what had happened almost five months prior was as clear-cut as I could imagine anyone giving me. It brought up my own sadness again, but at the same time he was connecting me to and talking with Jenny, and that trumped every other feeling.

Corey continued the conversation as if we were talking about my taxes—no weird staring off into space, nothing like I'd seen portrayed in films. He brought up several things that were evidentiary, some of which I didn't realize were so until later.

At one point he asked, "Have you seen the little beagle yet?"

I said, "No, we don't have any beagles in the cottage community where we live in Maine."

He clarified, "It's a small dog with floppy ears."

A little annoyed, I said, "I know what a beagle is; I had one growing up from fifth grade until I got married. But we don't have any. I pretty much manage the dog park in our little cottage community, and we have golden retrievers, a border collie, and some mutts, but I've been laying new wood chips in the park the past few weeks and have never seen a beagle there."

Corey said, "Well, just remember I mentioned it, and Jenny says when you see the little beagle, know that she is with you there."

He also asked if I ate at the Cracker Barrel much—that she wanted me to know she would be with me when I'm there. We always stayed overnight in our RV at Cracker Barrels instead of campgrounds for several reasons, not the least of which is that when we woke up in the morning, there was our breakfast: Big Momma's Pancake Special, warm and ready. Whenever we were on the road, Cracker Barrels were "home." They had parking big enough for the RV and seemed to welcome RVs.

Corey next said that Jenny wanted me to get outdoors and hike. I said, "No, I don't think so. I have plantar fasciitis, and she should know that I can't really hike anymore."

"Well, maybe walk more then, I don't know, but what's coming to me is *hike*."

Mary left the next day, Tuesday, July 25. On the way home from dropping her off at the Portland airport, driving southbound on I-95 to Wells, a car passed me with a license plate that read simply: "HIKE-J." I was floored and took a photo of it, but I'm not allowed to publish it here.

On Wednesday evening, I was laying some more wood chips the cottage owners had donated to the dog park, and Trek and Muf'n charged over to the entrance to sniff a new dog coming in: yep, a little beagle with floppy ears.

I was taken aback because we had lived in this cottage community for two summers and I'd never seen a beagle there before, or anywhere else on the property. I went over to see who it belonged to, and it was the wife of one of the people running for the new board. They lived at the very front of the property in the all-season section. Their cottage is about as far from the dog park as it could be, down by Route 1, but she'd heard I was refurbishing the playing surface and had come up to the rear, closer to Route 95, to see the park, probably for the first time. Fascinating.

Since there is no space and time on the other side, the folks there can apparently see things we have not experienced yet. In seminary I read that while we see life frame by frame as in a film clip, God sees it all on the entire reel. That's the best way I can find to explain this. There's still so much I can't explain.

I continued seeing different mediums almost as a kind of research project, trying to make sense of everything. What had begun as a search for answers about Jenny's death was now becoming a search to understand more about all of our lives and deaths. Did the mediums tell me pretty much the same thing? Were some better than others? What are their percentages of accuracy? (Generally, as a rule of thumb, even the best are only about 90 percent accurate.) The loved one in spirit has to communicate with the medium in symbols, and the medium receives and interprets the symbols to the sitter in ways he or she can understand. I was elated to keep hearing from Jenny in the process, but it was also becoming fascinating, as person after person, who didn't know Jenny or me, recounted similar facts, scenarios, and historical references. This was way beyond any information that could just be searched online, which skeptics assume is the case.

I met one medium, Katie, at a psychic fair where several metaphysical healers gathered and offered their specialty services. Katie, a young holistic nurse in Massachusetts, had a childlike innocence, even though she was a mom, and we really connected. She was the first medium who brought in my dad while Jenny stayed in the background for the first half of the reading. She said at first my dad wasn't sure he was welcome and asked if I wanted to hear from him. I said, "Sure," so she continued listening to him. He apologized for the way he had treated me, saying (and Katie clarified, "This is in no way, shape, or form an excuse") that he wanted me to know he also was abused as a child, and "if he had known better, he'd have done better" as a parent. That was very moving for me, and tears filled my eyes. Before his death, we had reconciled about a few hurtful experiences we needed to process together, but there were so many more we never got into during his physical life. I was glad he showed up.

Katie came up to Maine again in the early fall right before I left for Florida, and this time I made an appointment ahead of time. This session was pretty funny at the beginning. Mediums often start out with a prayer to request that only the highest and best come forward, so she began by holding my hand and praying quietly along those lines. This is not weird at all; it's like a simple, spontaneous prayer and more genuine than many I've heard from pastors over the years. The medium is not looking up to heaven or trying to be spiritual.

After a short pause, she said, "I have Jenny here and … Was she ordained or a spiritual person or something? Because I'm getting 'Rev.'"

You're not supposed to give any information, so I remained quiet. Then there was a longer pause while she concentrated again, trying to grasp the symbols Jenny was communicating—just the way people in normal conversation look when they're trying to remember a fact or name. She asked, "Did Jenny kind of keep you in line or something? I just keep getting 'Rev.'"

This cracked me up and became one of those "RV tire" moments in my journey that no one ever could have made up or guessed or been faking.

When we moved to Florida, driving was a challenge. We sold our motorcycles and tried to be careful driving in this new state where 80 percent of the population is over fifty and losing peripheral vision—and we were becoming senior drivers ourselves. I often did the driving since I had been a courier for a while before Jenny retired. I'd put on one hundred thousand miles without incident, so I felt confident on the road. It was one place where it felt my intuition was fired up and worked. For instance, when anyone cut in front of me, I could often tell that was about to happen and keep us safe. We had agreed to talk to each other, not to other drivers, about the times when that didn't work and we almost got hit. At those times, when I blurted out some unspiritual remark in the car, Jenny would calmly admonish me, "Now, Rev!" in her most schoolmarm tone of voice. It still amazes me that they still have their same personality and their same sense of humor.

I got back to Florida in early November, the day before my long-awaited appointment with Mike by

Skype. This became the day when I knew and believed that Jenny was with me in our house all of the time. It was an unbelievable hour on the phone.

Mike had the appearance and voice of a very young man, maybe twenty-five or so, whereas everyone else I had seen was older. I hate to be a reverse ageist, but honestly, what can a person in their twenties teach someone in their seventies about anything?

Well, he started by telling me Jenny had come to him as he was getting ready that morning and had spoken to him about us. Judith had told me the same thing back in June, so I understood that happens. But then he launched right into evidentiary material.

"Jenny wants to know if you remember a purple lounging jacket she gave you once."

I had no memory of this and responded, "No, I don't think so. We never gave each other things like that."

Mike said, "Well, Jenny is very insistent. She says it was dark purple, had kind of a satin finish, and she's very descriptive of the shiny fabric."

Bingo! It popped into my head. "Wow, Mike, that was back in 1994! That was downsized to Goodwill decades ago."

Back when we were entering all that data into her little Apple computer, it was taking so many hours that I even brought my dog up to her house, so Taupey wouldn't be alone for so long. In those days, jeans weren't made with spandex, and the work involved a lot of sitting. I have pictures of Jenny sitting on the floor in the family room, surrounded by papers and files, and wearing this turquoise lounging jacket with yoga-style pants. She had bought me a similar jacket in purple.

But that was so long ago, and I had no memory until she, through Mike, described it to a T.

This boggled my mind. I had no doubt that this was authentic communication from Jenny, but how do our loved ones describe something while no longer having eyes and ears? I was still in kindergarten here!

I was so excited. I was so sure now that he was chatting with Jenny and relaying everything to me, as if she were in our house and he was eavesdropping, that I used my iPhone to show him different pictures of Jenny and see if this is what she looked like to him. My kids had made a couple of 16-by-20-inch framed photos from our trips to Acadia with the dogs, and they were hanging around the house.

Mike said, "Jenny says if you're going to be showing me pictures, show me the picture of your (Lake Gaston) lake house. Did you guys live on a lake or something because she says that was her favorite house of everywhere you lived?"

Well, I didn't actually still have a picture of that house, but I was blown away that we could even be having this conversation. No one except me ever knew that fact. She so loved our lake house. It was twenty-five hundred square feet, and we built it with everything in mind—handicap-accessible bathrooms, bedrooms on the first floor, etc. (as if we still would be schlepping Jet Skis onto trailers when we were eighty-five years old). So that was our private joke, and it cracked me up. We had thought of everything in its design, except for the fact that we probably wouldn't be there in our old age. This was like a physical phone conversation.

Before we hung up, Mike asked if I had any questions, so I put my ignorance on the line, as I knew this was going to be my best chance to ever understand how this all worked. I asked him, "What do you see from where you are on the other side of this phone? Is Jenny here or what?"

He replied immediately, "Yes! She's right there over your right shoulder. She says she spends a lot of the time in your kitchen. Do you cook a lot or what?"

I said, "No, not cooking anymore, but in this house the kitchen is definitely central to the floor plan, very open, and is on the way to everywhere else, so that makes sense."

This was probably one of the most life-changing hours I had ever spent on the phone. As of November 7, 2017, I knew for sure that Jenny was there with me—not just in my heart or memory—I mean there in the house and in the car, relaying to me that the dogs still barked annoyingly in the car, everything she used to hear when she was here and had ears. I was still in kindergarten here, but Mike sends people a recording that tries to explain this all—vibration and so forth. It's about forty-five minutes long, and I would say it moved me from kindergarten to about third grade.

Basically, everything vibrates, and even solid things are always in motion molecularly. You don't have to have ears and eyes to pick up those vibrations and "hear" or "see" what's going on. Mediums are extremely sensitive to frequency and vibration, so they can pick up and connect with those on the other side in this way—much like we can pick up and connect with a radio station if we are tuned to that frequency, but if you want an FM station, you can't be dialing in to an AM station and vice versa.

The mediums I've met seem to believe that we each can learn to tune in to the frequency of our loved ones in this way—not that we can pick up *everyone's* vibrations but certainly those of our own loved ones. This became my new goal: learn to sense and feel energy in order to stop needing intermediaries to connect me with Jenny. We'll see about that!

CHAPTER 8
Other Settings and New Approaches

About an hour north of my house is a metaphysical church, Sarasota Center of Light, which holds its version of "Psychic Saturday" on the first Saturday of each month, just as in other places. I wanted to go to this program because I had met Katie at such an event in Maine, and she was excellent.

Here, I met Karin, who was a young mother of twins and quite friendly and easy to talk with. Again, sitting at one of several tables placed around the church's Fellowship Hall, she began by asking my full birth/maiden name and saying a prayer that only our highest and best good be served with any information coming forward. This time, my oldest sister, Diane, who was thirteen years older than me and had died in 2001, came in. She had come in with Corey too up in Massachusetts but just briefly, and at that time I was only focused on hearing from Jenny.

"Who is Lee?" Karin asked. Diane Lee was her name. My dad had named my oldest sister (as well as his sporting goods store) after some friend of theirs named Lee Fish, long before my time.

Later, the conversation turned to Jenny, and Karin asked if we had taken trips out west because Jenny was showing her images of Sedona and maybe Alaska. I said, "Yes, all of the above."

At one point, Karin said, "I have … It looks like a picture … It looks like a little Indian girl. Did you two sit in ceremony?" What she then described was a picture that Jenny woodburned and then painted in a class we took in Evart, Michigan, during the summer of 2008.

Jenny's attention to detail really paid off in woodcarving, wood burning, and painting. She had given this woodburning to our Virginia neighbors a few years ago, and it hung in their bathroom. They were now, like the rest of us, downsizing to a smaller lifestyle and location, and I had asked if I might have it back because they were letting go of some of their wall decorations. They understood its meaning to me, and on this particular morning, we had been texting about it, and Lois said she'd send it back to me.

So that's the image Jenny was showing Karin. I asked, "Are they listening when we are texting and sending emails?"

She replied playfully, "Yes, they're right there when you're hitting the 'send' button!"

I continued to drive up occasionally for the various programs this church offered—"What is Metaphysical Spirituality?" and "Shamanic Healing"—and to a few Sunday services. One of the mediums has a PhD in cultural anthropology and understands shamanic healing. That carries a lot of weight with me because I have such skepticism about energy work—Reiki, shamanic healing, past-life regression—and I'm wary of its abuses, so I would only be able to really learn from someone whose training I respected.

A month later, on December 28, I had my appointment with Madilyn by phone, from up north where she lives to Florida where I am most of the year. It's important to clarify that, in all of this, it matters not where you or the medium are physically; it's all about energy. Therefore, mediums don't need to know your last name, your email address, or your physical address. They don't need to know you or the person with whom you're connecting. In fact, the less they know about you and your life, the better it works. It truly is all about the energy they're "reading"; hence, this is why the sessions are called readings.

Madilyn called exactly at the appointed time. Once again, she had never met or heard of me, never met or heard of Jenny, and had no idea about anything. These readings often start off with small talk about the wonderful Florida weather compared to wherever the medium is, but very shortly rapport is established.

The biggest thing I remember about this conversation is that it was right after Christmas when it was my turn to host my four kids and ex-husband, Ed, who were visiting for the holidays, and I had been giving the grandkids most of Jenny's jewelry.

Madilyn said, "Were you giving away some of Jenny's things? Because Jenny was there as you were giving her jewelry to the grandkids the other day, and she's happy you are doing that, but she would like you to keep and wear the necklace with the letters and the crystal necklace."

I knew what the crystal necklace was because that was the one I had joked about decades ago, asking her not to wear it around me. But what was the "necklace with the letters"? I went over to where we'd all been looking at Jenny's jewelry.

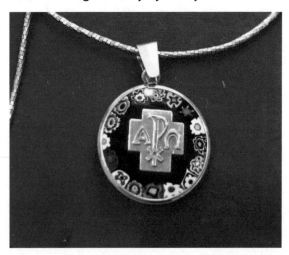

It was probably a First Communion necklace from long ago, with the Greek letters alpha and omega engraved in the center. Of course, she would want me to keep that one. And I had. But how did Madilyn get that message?

Next, she asked me something I thought was strange at the time. "Did you and Jenny used to look at the moon and stars?"

I was thinking, *What?*

She repeated the question.

"No, I don't think so," I replied. We were pretty busy with jobs and my kids and our dogs, so we really didn't have time to be sitting around looking at the moon and stars.

Two days after this reading, I was driving and listening to a Jane Olivor tape that Jenny had made for me of her favorite songs back in the fall of 1993. There was one I had been playing over and over in the car called "I Believe in You." The song describes believing in someone "just like the moon and stars that shine above; no matter where I go or what I do, within my heart, one thing is true: I still believe in you." I had been listening to that song repeatedly for the entire holiday season. It dawned on me that Jenny was conveying to me through Madilyn that she knew I was listening to our old Jane Olivor tape. It was another one of those mind-bending experiences.

I had heard that Madilyn was an excellent medium and that people from all over the world seek her out, but this was overwhelming. It's not that I was skeptical; I was just overwhelmed at the magnitude of what all this means for people—not just for me.

Madilyn also mentioned in this hour that Jenny said whenever I saw a cobalt-blue car to know that she was near me. I asked, "Did she actually *say* 'cobalt blue'?" And Madilyn affirmed, "Yes, cobalt blue, right here in front of me like on a Post-it note in front of my face." Cobalt blue was Jenny's favorite color, and I had discovered it was mine as well, once I knew it had a name. It's royal blue with a little purple in it, and

I had been noticing cars that color everywhere lately—parked next to me at Subway, at the pump at gas stations, and in my way while trying to pull out into traffic.

It's easy to dismiss those kinds of synchronicities by deciding cobalt blue was Ford's color du jour. Those are the things you'll never know, but it does give pause when five of them show up as you're driving by.

Back in May, when I first drove the RV from Florida to Maine, a car passed me with the license plate "SWIMR." When my son Aaron was thirteen, he set up an AOL email account for me, and he created a second account for me: SWIMR922. Since I never used the account, SWIMR922 became Jenny's screen name once we combined households. So SWIMR driving past me on I-75 was about Jenny? How likely is it that the only license plate with SWIMR on it—with one M and no E—is on the car that drives past me while I'm in the next lane on I-75?

I don't believe (yet) that every sign or license plate we pass has some deep personal meaning, but I do think that, statistically, it's not a high probability that SWIMR and HIKE-J were on the same road in the same ten seconds I was there without some kind of meaningful synchronicity.

The other thing I distinctly remember about my reading with Madilyn was that she asked, "Did you and Jenny used to argue about writing pens"? That was unbelievable because we did, though it was all in jest—except when it wasn't. Jenny preferred a specific kind of fine-point ballpoint pen to do her record-keeping, and just in general, because she had tiny writing and did a lot of figures and detail work. I always ended up grabbing one out of the junk drawer to write down a phone message and put it in my pocket. The next time she wanted it, it was wherever I last laid it. So, we created two junk drawers in the kitchen, and all her stuff was in her own drawer. Then I went to Staples and bought her a ten-pack of these pens with the grid on the grip so she would never be without one. Yet somehow when the landline rang, if her pen was lying near the phone, I'd pick it up and … déjà vu.

So, they weren't really arguments but more like when someone you live with leaves the cap off the toothpaste. Not a big deal, but to have it come up in a reading verified that Madilyn was talking to Jenny Young because how many other people ever heard about such an inconsequential part of our life together?

Madilyn concluded by saying that Jenny missed the tree she had tried so hard to save by digging around its roots at Seaglass Village, the community in Maine where we built our cottage in 2014. That is something no one but the two of us knew anything about. The builder had backfilled the roots of our stand of oak trees, and they were beginning to die at the top, so Jenny tried to free the roots that year.

Madilyn ended with "Is there a Mary? Jenny says, 'Say hi to Mary'." Mary was coming down to Florida again and had scheduled her visit during the week of the anniversary of Jenny's death.

This reading goes down in my chronology in the same category as Mike's Skype reading—undeniable evidentiary material that was clearly a direct connection with Jenny. Eventually you let go of having to understand it all and just accept it. It took me a long time to arrive there.

CHAPTER 9
A Grown-Up Cosmology

I want to point out some truths that I have discovered on this journey because they can be helpful and instructive but also confusing or even upsetting to seekers. Paul Tillich, a prominent Lutheran theologian, wrote a famous book of sermons decades ago called *The Shaking of the Foundations*. This is that. Grief is destabilizing enough, but then to discover that there actually is no death is even more so.

First of all, on the plus or positive side, these new understandings have clarified the entire meaning of the Christian faith, John 3:16, and Christ's resurrection for me in a way that I never had internalized despite seven years of seminary in Lutheran and Methodist communities, working for many years in the Cursillo movement with a Roman Catholic base, and attending the Spiritual Formation Academy of the United Methodist Church, as well as training in spiritual direction.

I now see that the women who experienced Jesus at Easter were connecting with him in exactly this way. Some other followers also were able to do that, and some were not. Those who did "see" him relayed what they were experiencing to others. Some followers believed their accounts and thus became the believers, some were doubters like Thomas was initially, and some simply did not believe—or did not want to believe because of the consequences for their own lives. But make no mistake: this is the *grown-up* cosmology the church should be teaching, not only to adults but also to children.

Above is a collage my ten-year-old grandson and his mom put together for me when Jenny died, and it depicts heaven and earth as separate places like we all pretty much learned in childhood. I was so touched by this collage, and I think it's a great cosmology for a ten-year-old, easy to grasp. That is, these *are* two pretty separate worlds. The problem is that most of us, as adults, have retained this picture of heaven and earth and still have a ten-year-old's cosmology. It is time for that thinking to grow up.

From not only my own but also others' experiences with mediums, who were able to connect us with our loved ones on the other side, it is clear that heaven is not "up there" or "out there"; it is a parallel reality running alongside this one but on a different frequency. Mediums and others, who can read and are sensitive to or tapped in to energy, can connect with the higher frequencies of those in that realm, or on the other side. That gets into vibration and quantum physics, the work of Joe Dispenza and Gregg Braden (see appendix). If you investigate that material, it will begin to come together (well, as much as is possible to understand in our physical form).

I took this same grandson, at age twelve, through the Bible in pictorial form when he flew up to Maine to spend a week with Grandma, and even a twelve-year-old was able to grasp the gist of everything I've written here—at his own level, of course.

Why would Christian teaching withhold this understanding even from adults, or discourage them from learning about it? What are we afraid of? No authentic theology can be based in fear. Here are my best guesses. I'm not a scholar anymore, and I don't approach the whole subject like that nowadays. In training for ministry, we learned four ways to discern spiritual truth: scripture, reason, tradition, and experience. What the church is underrepresenting today, I believe, are people's real-life experiences in this realm.

CHAPTER 10
Keeping Personal Boundaries in Spiritual Seeking

Where do mediums' abilities come from? That is something I was not concerned about initially, but it is something into which I have gained some insight. I have met many mediums now through personal readings and psychic fairs; through conferences at Kripalu in western Massachusetts, where they were presenting; and from sitting with them during meals for a week in the summer of 2018 at the Omega Institute in Rhinebeck, New York, where I was taking a course on increasing your intuition. A friend of mine had signed up for an advanced certification course for mediums, and I found myself dining with eight to ten of the mediums in that class, partly because of logistics and partly because I found their conversations fascinating. I was able to track with them pretty well, and they accepted me. Most of them could be stand-up comedians; they each had a great sense of humor.

From all of these encounters I have had with mediums over two years now, I learned that many of those I've met had experienced pretty horrendous childhoods—growing up with alcoholism, with physical or sexual abuse, and in various kinds of dysfunctional families. I'm not saying all mediums have experienced this, but many whom I have met had these kinds of "challenges," as one labeled them in a 2018 radio interview with the Forever Family Foundation.

So, is this a gift that God/Source/Universe gives them to help offset some of the dysfunction they have to work through in their lives? Is it a way to help them find meaning and purpose after some devastating circumstances? I don't know, of course. Maybe no one does.

But these mediums are on their own journeys, just as you and I are, to work out their psychological and personal integration. Just because they can be extremely tapped in to Spirit/God/Universe and pick up the high vibrations of those who have crossed over does not mean they are personally, psychologically, or spiritually integrated themselves. And you cannot expect them to be. That may seem like an oxymoron to some readers, who consider such people very close to God, but it is just one of the truths we have to accept.

It is extremely important that if you choose to consult a medium to connect you with your loved ones, carefully setting boundaries—yours and theirs—is crucial. It must remain a professional relationship. No matter how close you feel to the medium after sharing the depths of your love for and relationship with your deceased parent, partner, child, friend, or other loved one, keep the boundaries of the professional medium/client relationship. This is a medium's job, but it is also your job. Remember that they are each personally involved in their own process of growing and evolving, and they may be anywhere along a continuum of personal maturity, or lack thereof, in their own lives.

Here are some general guidelines to consider if you wish to pursue a connection with your loved ones through mediumship:

Waiting Period

It is generally advised to wait at least three months after your loved one has crossed over before consulting a medium. This is for several reasons. First of all, when we are in heavy, deep grief, our ability to hear is blocked somewhat (if not largely so), and it is not productive time spent. Secondly, when we are in deep grief, we are more vulnerable to any one of a number of dysfunctions that may show up if a medium is not yet "solidified" in his or her mediumship.

It is sometimes common for mediums—as they come into the public eye and realize they have skill and begin doing this for others—to explore various side trails, dabble in this piece on the journey, or look over there at that piece. Some may come out of this exploration phase a better and more well-rounded medium; others may get personally or psychologically sidetracked along the way, especially if they are not open to supervision or direction, and that can be a problem. Childhood abuse can result in complex PTSD, and this will always require some kind of therapy. Mediums who think they can talk or think themselves healed from such abuse are only fooling themselves.

Once again, as in so many other areas, moderation is probably the key. Spiritual seeking without good boundaries on the part of both the medium and the sitter is not where we want to be. And frankly, seekers in deep or recent grief are not usually playing with a full emotional deck, perhaps for quite some time.

Do Your Research

Choose the medium carefully: do your homework, choose authentic and certified mediums who have done their own personal work, and be willing to pay what they're worth. In that respect it's no different from having your roof worked on. You'll get what you pay for. And there is good reason to be bonded and insured. Sticking with certified mediums will also keep you away from con artists who claim to be mediums but are not. You can get referrals from friends whose own experience you know and trust. You can assess websites, looking for indicators of competence, professionalism, ethics, and red flags. Forever Family Foundation has a list of mediums it has certified through a rigorous process.

Record Your Sessions

It is really helpful to record your sessions, as you will be surprised at what was said three days or three weeks or three months ago that you don't remember ever hearing. Most mediums will allow this, and if not, ask why. Tied to this same idea, it's extremely useful to journal afterward about your sessions—your insights, thoughts, and feelings. Include especially the dates because you will realize that it all makes sense once you see the sequence of events—what a medium said maybe made no sense at the time, but then it evolved on such and such a date.

Keep a Journal of Your Spiritual Learning

You will learn through this experience more about the departed loved one's journey and *your own* than you could have known otherwise. For instance, I learned that we here on the physical plane can "hold on" to them in a way that is not helpful to their transition, and this is why the Universe sometimes arranges that we are not there when they pass. That is probably the reason I did not make it to the hospital at the time of Jenny's passing.

I have a new understanding of angels and spiritual guides that I had given up back in childhood and since then have resurrected. If you really want to learn, there will be no limits, and you need to write down and sort out what you learn, which leads me to the last guideline.

Find a Mentor You Trust

I have learned as much about God/Source/Universe in the past two years as I did in seven years of seminary training. It is an entirely different kind of learning but nonetheless life changing, and, in my opinion, it requires some mentoring or direction just as much as that which I received in seminary.

Spiritual seeking, especially in these times, is not child's play, and I can understand why some churches and other organizations try to control or limit it. It depends on the seeker: How much personal maturity do you have? How much are you able to self-regulate? How well do you discern the energy around you as well as your own? In my experience, the caveat is not about ghosts and spirits and bogeymen; none of the mediums I have seen have been bothered by those. But you *will* be swimming in strange new waters, and I am a huge advocate of having a coach or mentor until you get your flippers.

In the Case of Suicide

A word about suicide while I'm passing along things I've learned at conferences. At one Forever Family Foundation event, an attendee asked one of the certified mediums during the question-and-answer session what happens with people who commit suicide? She responded that they initially go to a kind of "special needs" class where they learn how that decision and action affected the loved ones they left behind. Another medium added that, for those who think they'd like to hasten their reunion with their departed loved ones, people should know that they may not end up where their loved one is, so that's not really a solution. Somehow there is "school" on the other side, where the departed still learn and are very busy! We may have very different lessons to learn from those we seek to be with.

CHAPTER 11
Claircognizance

Shortly before I returned to Florida in the fall of 2018, I had a phone reading with a new medium I had met briefly through the Forever Family Foundation (FFF) grief healing events. I wanted a medium who was certified through a strenuous process, and I understood that FFF only certifies about 10 to 15 percent of those who ask to be certified. I had sat in on a small group breakout session at a summer retreat, and I related well to this medium's presentation. I felt that she would understand my remaining and still-unanswered questions.

For this reading, I was in Maine and Amy, the medium, was in Georgia. I had learned along the way that phone readings were just like in-person readings since they are all done through energy. Amy didn't want any information at all, not even my last name.

I needed to clarify some of the confusions that had piled up about so many of my new learnings, and there was no one to help me process them as I had in seminary. So, I signed up for a medium reading for the first half hour and a psychic reading for the second half hour. Since those are two different things, she broke the time into two distinct segments to avoid confusion about the source of the information.

Amy began the medium portion by saying that Jenny was showing her some woodcarvings we'd done in the cottage where I was sitting, and they were scattered around the cottage. There was one bank of about five or six of them across one wall above a transom, and the third one in that line was off-kilter. "Jenny wants you to know she's doing that—messing with it—so you'll know she's there in the cottage with you."

I went into the great room and looked back over the transom of the sliding glass doors out to our sunroom where I had been sitting. There was the bank of our carvings, and the third one was off.

Amy continued the mediumistic reading, saying that she only sees past lives when they are relevant to the person sitting before her. "Michele, looking at the two of you, what I see here is … Jenny is showing me like a *list* of them. It's like if you were to take … you know how people used to put pictures in their wallet and lay them out like a foldout kind of thing? Jenny showed me like—I could barely count them—seven or eight lifetimes together, and in each one there were differences. You know, sometimes we're male, sometimes we're female, sometimes we're young, sometimes we're older … It's not like you were married in each one; there *was* one … there is a past life where you two were married … but you guys don't even have the same skin color, so it's a different race even. And that does happen. But this is why the pull between you two was so strong. You two were almost like magnets. It was so easy, and that's part of what I feel, unfortunately for you, is what you're missing.

"But you see, this is what it means to have a good soul connection. Obviously, we have many soul connections, not just one soul mate, but when we have one like this—when it's so many lifetimes—you can make agreements and do things without even talking. It's just so *easy* between two people …"

So, Jenny and I literally had been soul mates. The first two or three mediums had said that about us, way back to Judith in June of 2017. Maybe I wasn't ready to hear it then, but this time I was. This explained why I had felt such a connection to Jenny in the very beginning, decades ago. Everything started making more sense. The depth of grief I had been feeling wasn't just about this life's particularities; this was about, at some level, recognizing the relationship we have had in many different settings and over several lifetimes. This was amazing. Everything finally made sense.

As we moved into the psychic portion of the reading, and as I felt my trust level deepening, I explained that I often get mixed messages from people, and I need to understand what's going on there. She explained to me that I have "claircognizance," one of the "clairs"—just like *clairvoyance* is when people "see" images in their minds' eye, and *clairaudience* is when people "hear" the message, just as we can hear what a church bell sounds like even though it's not ringing right now. Claircognizance is "clear knowing". I *know* things that drop in on me; it's not that I think them. They're coming from what I call God. God has been so re-created in man's image that for many people that doesn't work as a descriptor anymore. So, if the word *Source* or *Universe* works better for you, we are really talking about the same One.

I told Amy that in a dream I had seen the Challenger on the bottom of the ocean a few days before that happened in January 1986. It looked like a saucerlike thing with chaise lounges arranged in pie-shape fashion. "Why," I asked, "would I be shown that if I had no power to change it or intervene?" It was something I had shoved down for the past thirty years and had wanted no part of, whatever it was called.

Amy said, "The problem with shoving claircognizance down is that, I would say, it represents about twenty percent of who you are, and when you do that, you're pushing away a significant part of yourself. It would serve you better to learn how to manage it and integrate it into your life."

Stated in this way, it sounded like a no-brainer all of a sudden.

So, this explained the mixed messages. I receive the truth of many situations (many intuitive people do; this is not unique to me). What this means is if I don't surround myself with extremely honest people who say what they mean and mean what they say, my life is going to be confusing because I will spend a great deal of time internally trying to reconcile the incongruence between what someone says to me and the truth I pick up. This was huge for me. It did mean stepping back from some immediate friendships in which I no longer thought those needs could be met. I was, however, able to trust the Universe that new friendships more compatible with who I am would fill the vacuum. I immediately—and I mean the very next day—felt more psychic energy available to me. Amy even had taken some time to explain how to know if that energy was coming from God or just from me by how and where I felt it in my body.

This conversation fits into my chronology as one of the most life-changing readings I have had. Basically, this medium saved me from myself, for which I will be forever grateful.

CHAPTER 12

Learning to Be Okay with Never "Understanding" It All

At the metaphysical church I occasionally attend, the pastor is also a medium. One month, the church was hosting the "First Saturday" event again, and I stopped by because my remaining sister had died a few months earlier, and I wondered if she would show up. Karin asked, at the end of my reading, "Do you paint at like a kitchen table looking out over some water or something? Because Jenny is showing me a picture of where you paint."

Painting has been what works best for me—along with staying connected to Jenny—to re-center myself and find my own truth. In the process so many memories are surfacing. We did a *lot* of fun things together, as well as all the learnings. We lived life. We prayed together for heart surgeries in children's hospitals, laid hands on babies we weren't sure would live, and celebrated weddings and births. And my truth that I hold clearly today is that I can grow to love someone deeply who I feel is very close to God, without respect to gender or race—those are not my criteria for love—and that love may be interrupted temporarily but will never die.

This has been a tremendously educational, fascinating, growth-producing, faith-generating journey, and I'm nowhere near the end. As a card that Jenny once gave me says, "There are no endings … only beginnings."

At this writing, I know Jenny is around me, and I talk to her. I still need intermediaries to hear her, however, though dreams are also starting to come back, and she did speak to me in one. My next work is becoming more sensitive to energy in general—my own as well as others'—and expanding my abilities to receive messages from Spirit without my intellect overriding them. Moving forward, I will be doing that with direction and mentorship. I now have one energy professional, a pranic healer, whom I trust, and I am learning so much that lines up exactly with what I've learned from the mediums.

I hope this book has opened you to the possibility that *your* loved ones are also right there with you—not just in your thoughts and your memory but actually there, right now, with you, in your home and in your car. Yes, it would be easier if they were physically here to join us for lunch and talk to without an intermediary. And grief does not automatically dissolve or resolve overnight by coming to these new understandings that our loved ones continue on in our lives. As Nora McInerny explains in a TED talk video on YouTube that is equal parts hilarious and poignant, "We don't move *on from* grief; we move *forward with* it." I recommend anyone who is grieving to watch this TED talk (https://youtu.be/khkJkR-ipfw).

If you have truly beloved ones whose passing was sudden and unexpected, I can think of nothing more comforting than to know that the message about eternal life they taught us in church is true and still operating today, and it's not for someday up the road; it's now.

"For God so loved the world, that he gave his only begotten Son, that whosoever believeth in him should not perish, but have everlasting life" (John 3:16 KJV). It's not just a quote for billboards and Bible thumpers; it's reality—our reality. And, as my professors at both Lutheran and Methodist seminaries taught us, "When you get to heaven, you'll discover it is an inclusive place for, and filled with, those who love. Because God is Love."

The Beginning

MISS JENNIFER ANN YOUNG

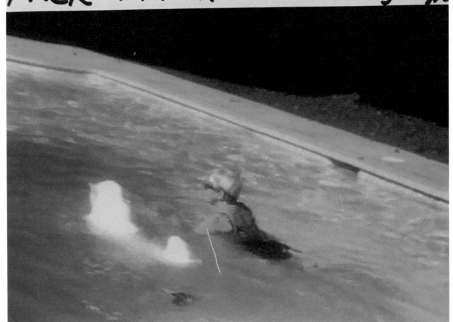

TReK + mom swimming 08/[...]

I am so grateful to Cynthia Schoenhoff, who was Jenny's friend before I met either of them. She taught Shakespeare and chaired the English department at the high school where Jenny was an administrator. Cyndee not only helped me edit this manuscript but also has been a real friend all along the way, from writing Jenny's obituary when I could not to helping me establish the Jennifer Ann Young Memorial Scholarship at their high school to encourage young people of integrity to pursue a career in education.

Our mutual friend and former parishioner, Mary Money, who is now a retired nurse and medical coder, helped me understand the medical jargon and charts, and Mary and Cyndee became fellow journeyers along the path to these afterlife discoveries.

Thank you to Gina Iacone and Brenda Quigley, also in Riverwood, for helping me to read our community's interest and organize the "Introduction to the Afterlife" events we offer quarterly. It is the community's response to those events that has helped me know this is not only my journey. I had fifteen chairs set up for the initial event until Gina said, "No, you need to go reset the room for fifty." And that is exactly how many people showed up. Who would have thought?

Thank you always, and again, to Dick Sweeney for just being there quietly in the background all these decades as I've grown at my own pace, and for being ready to step back in when I'm over my head. And much gratitude to my more recent mentors, Jill Willard, Amy Utsman, and Nancy Scheel, who each materialized in my life at the time when all of this needed to stop rattling around in my head and be put down on paper, as well as integrated into my body and heart.

Last but not least, I am grateful for Cathy and Duane Aldridge, who stepped in after Jenny crossed over to help me with our three Samoyeds, and for Jane Ann Emmel, who took our puppy, Trek Jr., to live with her and Tim in Georgia and handled TJ through to his Grand Championship, as we would have done. Without all of their help, I could not have continued the lifestyle Jenny and I shared.

Seriously, thank you all for the parts you have played. It takes a village!

—Michele and Jenny

"Love Decides*"
by Jane Olivor

Sometimes love decides for you…
and even when it makes no sense, well that's not up to you.
It's true, sometimes love decides for you.
…
No one knows why it comes and goes or where it's gonna lead,
Can't control who will touch your soul, who will stay and who will leave.
Love decides the one you'll find and if it's meant to be … It's true: Some things love decides;
Sometimes love decides for you.

---

* Sung by Jane Olivor, words by Marsha Malamet and Liz Vidal

Appendix

Forever Family Foundation Grief resources link:

www.foreverfamilyfoundation.org

Click on Grief and Loss on the drop-down menu on left, then click on "A Two Step Journey Through Grief" and the recommended books are listed in the order in which it is helpful to read.

In addition:

The books and websites of Joe Dispenza and Gregg Braden.

Drjoedispenza.com

www.greggbraden.com

Printed in the United States
By Bookmasters